DANCE
A First Look

KATIE PETERS

GRL Consultant, Diane Craig, Certified Literacy Specialist

Lerner Publications ◆ Minneapolis

TABLE OF CONTENTS

Dance

Dance is a fun sport. There are many kinds of dance.

People dance
to music.
The music can
be slow or fast.

What kind
of music do you
like to dance to?

I stand on my toes.
I bend my knees.
I leap into the air.

I step and jump.
I move my hips
and arms.

I spin and kick.
I run and stretch.

What dance moves do you know?

Tap shoes make loud
sounds when I dance.
Soft shoes are quiet
when I dance.

We go to class.

We learn new steps.

We dress up
for our show.
We dance on
a stage.
Our families watch.

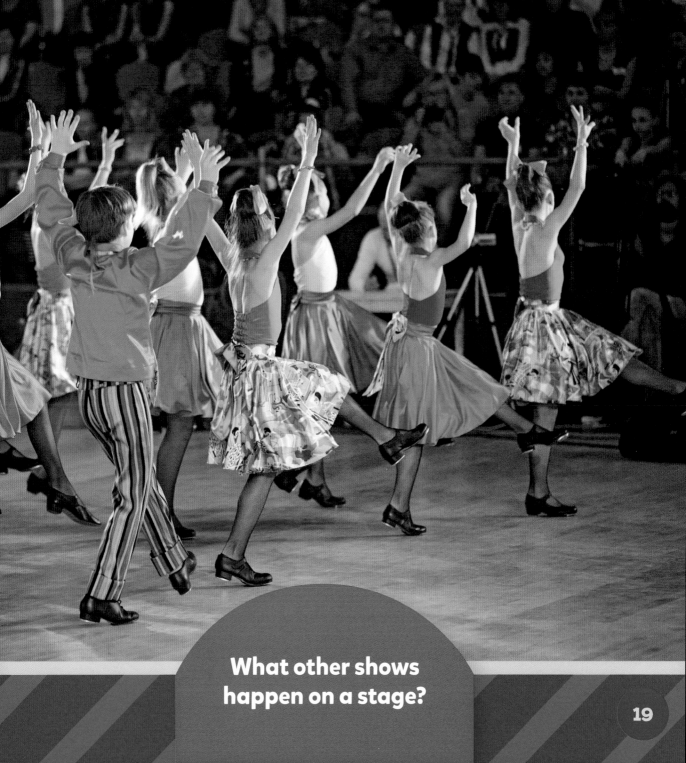

What other shows happen on a stage?

We move to the music.
We love to dance!

You Connect!

Have you ever gone to a dance class before?

What about dancing seems most fun to you?

How could you get better at dancing?

Social and Emotional Snapshot

Student voice is crucial to building reader confidence. Ask the reader:

What is your favorite part of this book?

What is something you learned from this book?

Did this book remind you of any sports you play?

Opportunities for social and emotional learning are everywhere. How can you connect the topic of this book to the SEL competencies below?

Responsible Decision-Making
Self-Awareness
Self-Management

Photo Glossary

leap

stage

stretch

tap shoes

Learn More

Allman, John Robert. *Boys Dance!* New York: Doubleday, 2020.

Howden, Sarah. *Misty Copeland: Ballet Star.* New York: HarperCollins, 2020.

Vanden Branden, Claire. *Dance.* Minneapolis: Pop!, 2020.

Index

Photo Acknowledgments

The images in this book are used with the permission of: © Hispanolistic/iStockphoto, pp. 4–5; © fizkes/iStockphoto, pp. 6–7; © gilaxia/iStockphoto, pp. 8–9, 23 (leap); © kali9/iStockphoto, p. 9; © Amorn Suriyan/iStockphoto, pp. 10–11; © Yagi-Studio/iStockphoto, p. 10; © adamkaz/iStockphoto, pp. 12–13 (both), 23 (stretch); © SpeedKingz/Shutterstock Images, pp. 14–15, 23 (tap shoes); © PeopleImages/iStockphoto, p. 15; © JackF/iStockphoto, pp. 16–17; © Pavel L Photo and Video/Shutterstock Images, pp. 18–19, 23 (stage); © FatCamera/iStockphoto, p. 20.

Cover Photograph: © Stígur Már Karlsson/Heimsmyndir/iStockphoto.

Design Elements: © Mighty Media, Inc.

Lerner Publications Company
An imprint of Lerner Publishing Group, Inc.
241 First Avenue North
Minneapolis, MN 55401 USA

For reading levels and more information, look up this title at www.lernerbooks.com.

Main body text set in Mikado a Medium.
Typeface provided by Hannes von Doehren.

Library of Congress Cataloging-in-Publication Data

Names: Peters, Katie, author.
Title: Dance : a first look / Katie Peters.
Description: Minneapolis, MN : Lerner Publications, [2023] | Series: Read about sports. Read for a better world. | Includes bibliographical references and index. | Audience: Ages 5–8 | Audience: Grades K–1 | Summary: "There are many different ways to dance. Jump into the basics in this engaging introduction to dance"— Provided by publisher.
Identifiers: LCCN 2022011564 (print) | LCCN 2022011565 (ebook) | ISBN 9781728475691 (library binding) | ISBN 9781728479026 (paperback) | ISBN 9781728484426 (ebook)
Subjects: LCSH: Dance—Juvenile literature.
Classification: LCC GV1596.5 .P42 2023 (print) | LCC GV1596.5 (ebook) | DDC 792.8—dc23

LC record available at https://lccn.loc.gov/2022011564
LC ebook record available at https://lccn.loc.gov/2022011565

Manufactured in the United States of America
1 – CG – 12/15/22